# Who Was Anne Frank?

By Ann Abramson

Illustrated by Nancy Harrison

PUFFIN

In memory of all the children who, like Anne,
had their life ended in that terrible war – A.A.

PUFFIN BOOKS

UK | USA | Canada | Ireland | Australia
India | New Zealand | South Africa

Puffin Books is part of the Penguin Random House group of companies
whose addresses can be found at global.penguinrandomhouse.com.

puffinbooks.com

Penguin
Random House
UK

First published in the USA by GROSSET & DUNLAP, Penguin Group (USA) Inc., 2007
This edition published in Great Britain by Puffin Books, 2016
001

Written by Ann Abramson
Text copyright © Grosset and Dunlap, 2007
Illustrations copyright © Nancy Harrison, 2007

The moral right of the author and illustrators has been asserted

Printed in Great Britain by Clays Ltd, St Ives plc

A CIP catalogue record for this book is available from the British Library

ISBN: 978–0–141–36574–9

# Contents

# Who Was
# Anne Frank?

## ANNE FRANK

Anne Frank's life was short. She was only
fifteen years old when she died in 1945.

She was born in Germany, where her father's family had lived for a very long time.

Her father was very proud of being German. He expected his children to live in Germany, and their children after them.

But that did not happen. The Franks' lives were turned upside down. They had to flee from their country. They had to go into hiding. They lost everything that was dear to them . . . all because they were Jewish and a man named Adolf Hitler was in power.

Hitler hated Jewish people. *All* Jewish people. By the time Hitler was defeated, Anne's mother was dead. So were Anne and her sister. The only person in the family who survived was Anne's beloved father, Otto.

But something else survived, too.

Anne's diary. Anne kept a diary for two years. Throughout that time, her family was in hiding from Hitler's soldiers.

Anne understood the dangers that her family faced. Yet in her diary she remained hopeful about the world, even though terrible things were happening. She drew comfort from the beauty of nature, even though she couldn't step outside for a single breath of fresh air.

After her death, Anne's diary was turned into a book.

ANNE FRANK

The Diary of a Young Girl

# ADOLF HITLER

ADOLF HITLER WAS BORN IN 1889. HE FIRST HOPED TO BECOME AN ARTIST, BUT HE WASN'T TALENTED ENOUGH – SO HE TURNED TO POLITICS INSTEAD. HIS DREAM WAS TO MAKE GERMANY THE MOST POWERFUL EMPIRE ON EARTH. GERMANS CALLED HITLER THE 'FÜHRER', WHICH IS THE GERMAN WORD FOR 'LEADER'. (YOU PRONOUNCE IT LIKE THIS: FA-YOUR-UHR.)

HITLER RULED OVER GERMANY FROM 1933 UNTIL 1945 WHEN, DURING THE LAST DAYS OF WORLD WAR II, HE KILLED HIMSELF RATHER THAN SURRENDER AND FACE TRIAL.

FROM THE START, HITLER CONVINCED GERMANS THAT JEWS WERE TO BLAME FOR MANY OF THE COUNTRY'S PROBLEMS. IN SPEECHES, HE WORKED GIANT CROWDS INTO A FRENZY BY SCREAMING THAT SOMETHING HAD TO BE DONE. ONE OF HIS ANSWERS WAS TO GET RID OF THE JEWS – ALL OF THEM. UNDER HIS DIRECTION, THIRTEEN MILLION PEOPLE WERE KILLED, SIX MILLION OF THEM JEWS.

HOW CAN A PERSON BE SO EVIL? THOUSANDS OF BOOKS HAVE BEEN WRITTEN ABOUT HITLER IN THE SEVENTY YEARS SINCE HIS DEATH, BUT NONE OF THEM HAVE REALLY FOUND AN ANSWER.

Today, more than seventy years after Anne's last diary entry, she remains a symbol of hope. Her diary has been translated into more than sixty-five languages. It has sold more than thirty million copies. There have been plays and films about her.

A short life – even a very short life – can be full of meaning.

# Chapter 1
# A Happy Home

Anne Frank was born on 12 June 1929, in the city of Frankfurt, Germany. Twelve days later, little baby Anne and her mother, Edith, came home from the hospital.

The Franks were like many other families of the time. Anne's father, Otto, was a businessman. Her mother stayed at home caring for Anne and Anne's older sister, Margot.

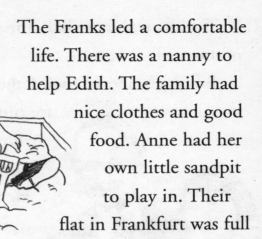

The Franks led a comfortable life. There was a nanny to help Edith. The family had nice clothes and good food. Anne had her own little sandpit to play in. Their flat in Frankfurt was full of books.

Otto Frank was many years older than his wife, and in lots of ways they were opposites. Otto was tall and thin; Edith was plump. Otto loved being around people. He was high-spirited and outgoing, while Edith was shy and quiet.

Otto loved to read to his daughters. He also made up wonderful stories at bedtime. Some were about two sisters named Paula. One of the Paulas was very well behaved and polite, like Margot. The other Paula was always getting into lots of trouble.

That Paula was more like Anne, who was full of mischief.

Both girls adored their father. Their nickname for him was 'Pim'. Besides telling stories, Pim loved to play games. He was also a very good photographer. He took many pictures of his girls and kept a photo album for Anne.

Anne was also very close to Edith's mother. She called her 'Oma', which means 'grandmother' in German. Oma loved spoiling Anne. Once when she was on a bus with Oma, Anne looked around and said,

'Won't someone offer a seat to this old lady?'
Anne was only four and a half at the time!
But that was Anne. She was always outspoken.

Her father understood her. He and Anne
were very much alike. Anne did not get along

nearly as well with her mother. They often had fights. Anne was jealous because she felt that her sister was her mother's pet. While Margot was serious and mild-mannered, Anne was moody and had a temper. But she was also lively and full of fun. Both sisters had dark shining hair, large eyes and lovely smiles.

The Frank family was Jewish. They followed certain customs and went to pray at their synagogue on important days. They celebrated some Jewish holidays, but not all of them. There were Jewish practices that they chose not to follow.

Many of Anne and Margot's friends in the neighbourhood were not Jewish. They sometimes came to the Franks' house to celebrate Jewish holidays such as Hanukkah.

Hanukkah menorah

Like all small children, Anne was not really aware of the bigger world around her. She knew her home, her family, her friends. That was her world. She did not know that Germany was going through many changes – many frightening changes.

World War I (known then as the Great War) had ended in 1918 with Germany's defeat. Unlike Otto Frank, many Germans were out of work after the war's end. And prices for everything – even milk and bread – were sky high.

A new leader came to power in 1933: Adolf Hitler. He was head of the National Socialist, or Nazi, party. Hitler made the Germans feel better about themselves. He said German people were smarter and better than any other people on earth. 'Pure' Germans, that is. Not Jews. In loud speeches before huge crowds, Hitler blamed Jewish people for many of Germany's problems.

# WORLD WAR I

WORLD WAR I, A TERRIBLE WAR THAT LASTED FROM 1914 TO 1918, WAS ALSO CALLED THE 'GREAT WAR'. THE CENTRAL POWERS (AUSTRIA-HUNGARY, GERMANY AND TURKEY) FOUGHT AGAINST THE ALLIES (RUSSIA, BRITAIN, BELGIUM, ITALY, FRANCE AND, LATER ON, THE UNITED STATES).

EVENTUALLY, THE ALLIES WON. GERMANY WAS FORCED TO PAY A LOT OF MONEY AS PUNISHMENT FOR ITS ROLE IN THE WAR. THIS LEFT THE COUNTRY VERY POOR AND MANY OF ITS PEOPLE VERY RESENTFUL. A NEW GOVERNMENT WAS SET UP – A DEMOCRACY. BUT IT WASN'T VERY STRONG. IN 1933, THE GERMANS LOOKED TO A DANGEROUS LEADER, ADOLF HITLER, TO MAKE THEIR COUNTRY GREAT AGAIN.

WORLD WAR I WAS ALSO KNOWN AS THE 'WAR TO END ALL WARS'. BUT UNFORTUNATELY, IT DIDN'T. WORLD WAR II BEGAN BARELY TWENTY YEARS LATER.

'Anti-Semitism' is a word that means 'hatred of Jews'. There was anti-Semitism long before Adolf Hitler, and in many places besides Germany. Throughout the world, at different times in history, Jewish people had to live in special neighbourhoods. They couldn't go to school with Christians or hold certain kinds of jobs.

But Adolf Hitler went much further.

His plan was to get rid of all Jews.

Of course, he did not say that out loud. Not at first.
But as soon as he came to power, he started making
life harder for German Jews like the Franks.

Hitler was dangerous. Otto Frank saw that. He decided that his family would be safer if they left Germany. It must have been a hard decision for Anne's father to leave home. He loved his country. He had fought for Germany in World War I. In 1933, there were more than 500,000 German Jews. In the next six years, more than half of them fled the country.

For a short time, the family lived with Anne's other grandmother in Switzerland. Then, in autumn 1933, Otto Frank moved to Amsterdam. By January 1934, the rest of the family had joined him there.

Amsterdam is the largest city in the Netherlands, a small country to the west of Germany. Why did the Franks pick this country? It was close, for one thing. And Otto already knew how to speak Dutch, the language of the Netherlands. But even more importantly, the people were known for getting along with everyone – including Jews.

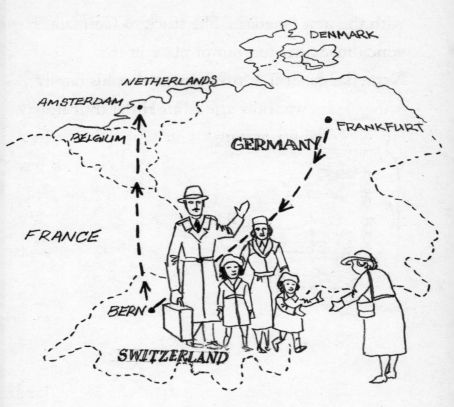

In Amsterdam, Otto started a new company, making pectin. Pectin is a powder used to make jam. The Franks moved into a flat in a block of new houses. The girls started school, and made new friends. Margot and Anne learned to speak Dutch very quickly. Only Edith had trouble with the new language. She stuck to German, which made her feel out of place in the Netherlands. Still, Otto thought that his family was now safe from Hitler. But he was wrong.

# Chapter 2
# A New Home

Amsterdam is a pretty city. It is filled with canals, and boats travel up and down them at all hours of the day. Anne was only four years

old when she moved there in 1934. Amsterdam quickly became her home.

The Franks' new flat was not as large as the one in Frankfurt, but it had room for guests. Otto and Edith missed their old friends and family. So they were very happy when Oma came to live with them. They hoped other relatives would visit, too. Many other Jewish families moved from Germany to Amsterdam, and the Franks soon had a circle of German-Jewish friends. At school, half the children in Anne's class were Jewish. Some had even come from Frankfurt, just like her.

Anne was a good pupil, although she hated maths. She was a chatterbox, and often teachers had to scold her to be quiet. In her free time she liked playing ping-pong. She started a ping-pong club called the Little Bear Minus Two Club. There were five members. The name of the club came from the number of stars in the Little Bear

constellation. Anne had thought there were five stars. But really there were seven, which explains the 'minus two' in the club's name.

Anne liked to read – history books and Greek myths and a popular series of books about a girl named Joop who was adventurous and lively like Anne.

Anne liked ice-skating and riding her bike with her friend Hanne. Hanne went along with all of Anne's jokes and games. Sometimes Anne

and Hanne stood on the
balcony of the Franks'
apartment and poured
water on the people in the
street below.

Anne was a good
swimmer. Amsterdam was
not far from the seashore.
Many photos show Anne
and Margot at the beach in
swimsuits. In one photo,
skinny little Anne has a
blanket wrapped around
her. She later wrote
that she had been
freezing when
the picture was
taken. Her
mother often
worried that
Anne would

catch cold because she was sick a lot. She missed many days of school because of coughs and flu.

She loved going to the cinema. Anne cut out pictures of film stars from magazines. She even had daydreams about being a film star herself one day. But she wasn't sure if she'd be pretty enough.

Anne always thought she was an ugly duckling.

In many ways, Anne's childhood was the same as lots of other children's. Except every once in a while, something scary would happen.

In 1938, her uncle Walter was arrested in Germany for being Jewish, and was sent to a labour camp. It was like a prison. Eventually Uncle Walter was lucky enough to win his freedom by agreeing to leave Germany forever. He ended up moving to the United States.

But how safe were the Netherlands?

# THE WHITE ROSE

NOT ALL GERMANS BELIEVED IN ADOLF HITLER OR HIS HATEFUL IDEAS. SOME RISKED THEIR LIVES TO STAND UP TO THE NAZIS. IN THE CITY OF MUNICH, A GROUP OF UNIVERSITY STUDENTS WROTE LEAFLETS AGAINST THE NAZIS THAT WERE GIVEN OUT ALL OVER GERMANY. THE LEAFLETS WARNED THAT HITLER WAS DESTROYING THE FREEDOM OF THE GERMAN PEOPLE. IT WAS TIME TO STAND UP FOR JUSTICE AND TOLERANCE.

SOPHIE SCHOLL

HANS SCHOLL

THE STUDENTS WERE LED BY A BROTHER AND SISTER NAMED HANS AND SOPHIE SCHOLL. THEY CALLED THEIR GROUP 'THE WHITE ROSE'. BUT THE NAZIS PUT AN END TO THE WHITE ROSE AND KILLED ITS LEADERS. TODAY MANY GERMAN SCHOOLS, STREETS AND LANDMARKS ARE NAMED IN HONOUR OF THE BRAVE YOUNG PEOPLE WHO WERE NOT AFRAID TO SPEAK OUT.

In 1938, Hitler reunited Austria and Germany. Austria was on the southern border of Germany. The people there spoke German, and most were happy to be part of this powerful empire.

They cheered Hitler's soldiers when they marched into the city of Vienna.

The Dutch, however, hated Hitler. Most people couldn't stand the idea of being under his control. But did it matter what they thought? In March 1939, Germany invaded Czechoslovakia. What if Hitler decided to make the Netherlands part of his empire, too?

Otto and Edith Frank had to make a hard decision. Should the family stay in Amsterdam or move again? And if they did move, where would they go? To England? To the United States? To a country in South America? It was very hard to get visas to live in other countries. Besides, Anne and her sister were happy in Amsterdam. And even though Edith was not, she liked knowing that her relatives in Germany were nearby. By 1939, Otto Frank was fifty years old. He felt that he was too old to start his life over yet again.

In the end, the Franks decided not to uproot the family for a second time. They would stay in Amsterdam.

# Chapter 3
# Another World War

After Hitler invaded Poland in September 1939, England and France declared war. This was the start of World War II. Italy sided with Germany. For the time being, the United States — an ocean away — stayed out of the conflict.

As for the little country of the Netherlands, it remained neutral. That meant it did not take sides. The Dutch hoped that this would keep Hitler's army away.

At night, over coffee and cake,

THE TIMES

HITLER INVADES POLAND

the Franks and other Jewish families in Amsterdam
talked about the war. Their dream was that Hitler

would be defeated. Then they could all return to
Germany. On the radio, they listened to the latest
news. But they never discussed their fears about
the future in front of the children.

The Franks continued with their daily lives.
They took family trips. One summer holiday
was spent at a seaside town in Belgium, and
they toured the canals of the Netherlands in a
houseboat one spring.

The first months of 1940 were bitterly cold.
Anne did not mind. The canals remained frozen
for much longer than usual, so she and her
friends spent many hours ice-skating. She was
ten and a half now and longed for real figure
skates. That way she could do jumps and other
tricks on the ice. All she had were Margot's old
skates. They were just blades that attached to
Anne's shoes with a key.

Her parents had no time to think about ice skates. They were worried about an attack on the Netherlands. There were many warnings about the Germans invading. But time and again the warnings proved to be false alarms.

Late that spring, the weather turned warm and sunny – and suddenly everyone's worst fear came true. On 10 May 1940, Germany invaded. Hitler had only been waiting for warmer weather to send in his planes. On the morning of the attack, bombs dropped from the sky. Amsterdam shook as if there had been an earthquake.

Two days later, more bombs fell on Amsterdam. The airport was on fire, as was the harbour. But Amsterdam was lucky. Another city, Rotterdam, had been destroyed. Thousands of people died.

The Queen of the Netherlands managed to escape to England, where she remained until the war was over. She stayed in touch with her people through radio broadcasts. The queen told everyone

to stay calm. But there was no telephone service. There were no buses or trains running. People

began to panic. Scared of running out of food, they bought out grocery stores. Soon shelves were empty. Air-raid alarms warning of more bombs sounded throughout the day. The people of the Netherlands were prisoners in their own country.

Some Jews in the Netherlands tried to leave the country by ferry, but very few people got out. The Franks did not even try to escape. They had no car, and Anne's grandmother was old and very sick. She could not travel.

Anne's parents had fled to Amsterdam to escape the Germans. But now the Germans had come to Amsterdam. There was no place left for Anne's family to run. Their only other choice was to hide.

# RESISTANCE

BANDS OF JEWISH FIGHTERS DID WHAT THEY COULD TO STOP THE NAZIS. THESE UNDERGROUND FIGHTERS WERE CALLED RESISTANCE FIGHTERS. OFTEN THEY WERE HELPED BY NON-JEWS.

THE MOST FAMOUS UPRISING WAS IN WARSAW, POLAND. DURING WORLD WAR II, JEWISH PEOPLE IN MANY CITIES WERE FORCED TO LIVE IN SEPARATE NEIGHBOURHOODS CALLED GHETTOS. THE LARGEST GHETTO WAS IN WARSAW.

BY 1943, THE JEWS IN THE WARSAW GHETTO HAD REALIZED THAT BEING SENT TO A CONCENTRATION CAMP WAS A DEATH SENTENCE. THEY ALSO KNEW THAT THERE WAS NO HOPE OF DEFEATING THE NAZIS. THEY HAD HARDLY ANY WEAPONS AND WERE TRAPPED INSIDE THE GHETTO, YET THEY CHOSE TO FIGHT ANYWAY. THEY MANAGED TO HOLD OUT AGAINST THE ENEMY FOR ALMOST A MONTH. OF THE 60,000 PEOPLE LIVING THERE, 7,000 DIED IN THE UPRISING. OF THOSE WHO REMAINED, 50,000 WERE CAPTURED AND SENT TO CONCENTRATION CAMPS.

TODAY THERE ARE MEMORIALS TO THE HEROES OF THE WARSAW GHETTO IN CITIES ALL OVER EUROPE AND THE UNITED STATES.

# Chapter 4
# Occupied!

The Netherlands was now an occupied country. That meant the Germans were in control. Up went Nazi flags. Right away, life

began to change for everyone, but it changed most of all for the Jews.

Now all Jews – even children like Anne and her sister – had to register with the Germans. Nobody else had to do this. But the Germans wanted to keep track of all Jews. They wanted to know who each person was and where he or she lived. Jews had to turn over nearly all their money to the Nazis. Their businesses were taken away. (Otto handed his over to two good friends who already worked there and weren't Jewish.) If Jews worked in companies owned by non-Jews, their jobs were taken away.

Books by Jewish authors were banned. So were films made by Jews. Jewish people were no longer even allowed to go to the cinema, which must have upset Anne a great deal. Her parents did all they could. They rented projectors and films to show at home. Anne and her friend Jackie made tickets and led people to their seats,

while Edith provided them with refreshments.

There were random attacks against Jewish people, too. One Saturday afternoon a group led by German soldiers beat up and arrested over 400 Jewish men. Otto was lucky enough to stay out of harm's way. The arrested men were sent to concentration camps. Only one of the men ever returned to the city.

The Dutch people were outraged. They staged a strike. At ten thirty one morning in February, work stopped all over the Netherlands.

Trams came to a halt. Shops closed. Restaurants
didn't serve food. Factories shut down. It was
a countrywide strike. In this way, the Dutch

people showed Hitler what they thought of him:
that his treatment of the Jews was wrong, unfair
and inhuman.

Did this stop the Germans? No.

By now there was no way for Anne's mother and father to keep what was happening from their children. Signs went up on park benches, marking them as 'Forbidden to Jews'. Jewish people in Amsterdam were no longer allowed in libraries, museums, concert halls, restaurants or even the zoo.

That summer Jews were forbidden to use public beaches and pools. They could not visit public parks or hotels. How awful for everyone, but most of all for children like Anne and her friends. It was the middle of summer and there was nowhere they could go to have fun.

Each time something was taken away from them, Jewish people hoped that nothing worse would happen. And indeed there were still happy times for the Franks. Anne spent part of her summer holidays with her friend Sanne's family in the country. It was while she was at Sanne's house that Anne first started noticing boys.

There was also a wedding. Everyone in the Frank family was very close to a young Dutch woman named Miep, who worked at the pectin company. She was not Jewish, and nor was her new husband, Jan Gies, but Miep had known and respected Otto Frank for many years. She was also especially close to Anne. Anne did not know it then, but soon this young couple was going to play a very important part in her life.

# Chapter 5
# Yellow Stars

The Nazis robbed Jewish people of their
rights, one by one. They also took pleasure
in making public spectacles of the Jews; they
wanted to shame them. In the summer of 1941,
the Nazis decided that Jewish children could
not return to their old schools. Now they would
have to attend separate schools for Jews only.

But instead of announcing the change over the summer, the Nazis waited until school started. Then Jewish students were publicly removed from their classes. It was another way to make them feel like outcasts.

At least Anne was in a class with her friend Hanne at the new school. And some things did not change . . . the teachers still scolded Anne for talking all the time!

In April 1942, the Nazis made all Jews over six years old start wearing a big yellow patch on their clothes, shaped like a Jewish star. The Jewish star, or the Star of David, is a six-sided star made from two triangles. It is the most common symbol of the Jewish religion. These stars had to be worn on overcoats, jackets and dresses. They were sewn right over your heart, where everyone would be sure to see them.

# THE STAR OF DAVID

ACCORDING TO LEGEND, THE STAR OF DAVID WAS ON THE SHIELD OF KING DAVID, A WISE AND HEROIC KING OF ISRAEL IN ANCIENT TIMES.

HITLER DECIDED THAT ALL JEWISH PEOPLE HAD TO WEAR YELLOW CLOTH STARS THE SIZE OF A GROWN-UP'S HAND. THIS WAS TO SINGLE THEM OUT. IN THE MIDDLE OF THE PATCH WAS THE WORD 'JOOD', WHICH MEANT 'JEW' IN DUTCH. IT WAS WRITTEN IN LETTERS THAT LOOKED LIKE HEBREW LETTERS. ALTHOUGH IT WAS MEANT TO BE A BADGE OF SHAME, MANY JEWS WORE THEIR PATCH PROUDLY.

IN 1948, SOON AFTER WORLD WAR II ENDED, THE NEW STATE OF ISRAEL WAS BORN. IT WAS CREATED AS A HOMELAND FOR ALL JEWS. THE STAR OF DAVID APPEARS ON THE BLUE-AND-WHITE FLAG OF ISRAEL.

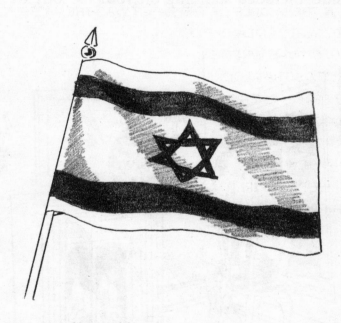

For some time Jews had not been allowed to own cars, but now they were forbidden to ride bikes as well. There was a curfew that said that all Jewish people had to be in their homes by eight o'clock at night. They could not go outside again until six o'clock the next morning. Being 'outside' included standing on your balcony or

sitting in your back garden. If you were caught where you weren't supposed to be, you were arrested – even children.

The only good news was that Hitler's forces were starting to lose ground in the war. The Germans had invaded France, but they were not able to invade England. Then, in December 1941, the United States joined the war. The Franks hoped that this meant that Hitler would soon be defeated. Then the nightmare would end and life could go back to normal.

# Chapter 6
## Kitty

The day Anne turned thirteen, in June 1942, one important person was not there. Oma had died that winter. Anne said that her birthday didn't mean much without her grandmother, but in the Frank family there was always a lovely

birthday party. This year Anne invited both boys and girls. Her mother baked a wonderful cake and her father screened a film about a brave dog named Rin Tin Tin.

This was the last real birthday party the Franks ever threw. Anne received many presents from her family: books, a jigsaw puzzle, a brooch and sweets. But there was one gift she treasured most of all. It was a small notebook with a red-and-green checked cover that locked. On the inside cover Anne placed a photograph of herself. Next to it she jokingly wrote, 'Gorgeous, isn't it?'

Anne named her diary 'Kitty' after an old friend with that name. Two days after her birthday, Anne made the first entry in her new diary. Every entry started with 'Dear Kitty . . .'

Anne told Kitty everything – all about a boy she liked, quarrels she had with her friends, books she had enjoyed. Everything. Kitty was a friend who never argued and always listened.

Less than a month later, there was terrible news to tell Kitty. One Sunday afternoon in early July 1942, a notice arrived in the mail. Margot was to be sent to a labour camp in Germany!

She was ordered to show up at the train station with her belongings and enough food for a three-day trip.

The Nazis had started rounding up groups of Jews for labour camps, hundreds a day. Edith had thought that Otto might be arrested, but never one of her daughters. Margot was only sixteen. The Germans had promised not to split up families.

No matter what, Otto and Edith were not letting their daughter be taken away. The only answer was to do what many other Jews were doing. The whole family had to disappear as soon as possible – the next morning at the very latest.

What Anne and her sister didn't know was that their father had already found a hideout. It was attached to the building where his company offices were. There was a secret stairway leading to a group of rooms.

# THE BACK OF THE SECRET ANNEX

For several months, Otto and Edith had been getting the hideout ready. Every night they moved in pieces of furniture, plates, silverware and bedding. They were careful to bring just a few things at a time. A bathroom with a toilet was built, and there was a stove in the hideout, too. What the Franks were doing was not unusual. By 1943 between 20,000 and 30,000 Jews in the Netherlands had gone into hiding.

That night, Margot and Anne packed their school bags with a few personal belongings. Anne put in curlers, hankies, books, a comb and a few letters. The girls were not told where they were going. Anne could not say goodbye to any of her friends. Otto left a note in the flat with an address in Switzerland scribbled on it. He wanted people to think the Franks had fled the Netherlands.

The next morning, the girls put on several layers of clothes under their raincoats. It was too dangerous to carry a suitcase. The family closed the door of the home they had lived in for eight years. Anne barely had time to hug her beloved black cat. Anne was sure she would be back home

soon and knew the neighbours would care for little Moortje. Still, her eyes welled with tears.

There was one more thing Anne made sure to keep with her. Safe in her school bag was her plaid cloth-covered diary, Kitty.

ANNE WORE TWO JUMPERS, THREE PAIRS
OF PANTS, A SKIRT, A DRESS, A JACKET AND A
RAINCOAT, SUMMER SHORTS, TWO PAIRS OF SOCKS,
HEAVY LACE-UP SHOES, A CAP AND A SCARF.

# Chapter 7
# The Secret Annex

What was it like to live in the hideout – or the Secret Annex, as it was called?

Firstly, the hideout was very small. Though over two floors, the entire space was only forty square metres. Behind the secret door were two rooms, one with a stove and sink, and the bathroom. The floor above had two more narrow little rooms, one for Edith and Otto, the other for Margot and Anne. Luckily Anne's postcards and film star photos were waiting for her.

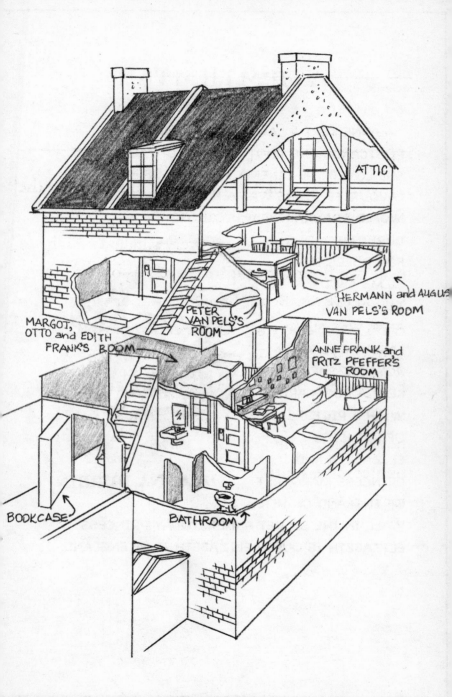

ATTIC

HERMANN and AUGUS
VAN PELS'S ROOM

PETER
VAN PELS'S
ROOM

MARGOT,
OTTO and EDITH
FRANK'S ROOM

ANNE FRANK and
FRITZ PFEFFER'S
ROOM

BOOKCASE

BATHROOM

# A FIRM FILM FAN

ANNE KEPT A LARGE COLLECTION OF
POSTCARDS AND PHOTOGRAPHS OF FILM STARS.
SHE LOVED THE CINEMA, AND ONE OF HER
FAVOURITE STARS WAS A HOLLYWOOD ACTRESS
NAMED DEANNA
DURBIN, FAMOUS
FOR ROLES IN
FILMS ABOUT
TEENAGERS.
ANNE WAS ALSO
FASCINATED WITH
ROYALTY. SHE
KEPT A POSTCARD
WITH A PICTURE
OF PRINCESS
ELIZABETH AND
PRINCESS MARGARET
OF ENGLAND ON HER
WALL IN THE SECRET ANNEX. TODAY PRINCESS
ELIZABETH IS QUEEN ELIZABETH II OF ENGLAND.

**DEANNA DURBIN**

ANNE SPENT A LOT OF TIME ON HER PHOTO COLLECTION AND WAS ALWAYS CHANGING MAGAZINE CLIPPINGS AND POSTCARDS TO KEEP THINGS INTERESTING AND UP TO DATE. THE LAST PICTURES SHE HAD ON THE WALL ARE STILL THERE.

Princess Elizabeth and Princess Margaret

Her father had brought the postcards beforehand. So Anne stuck up as many as she could on the bare walls to make the room look more cheerful.

Food supplies were stored in the attic, which had two small windows. From one window Anne could see a tall clock tower. From the other was a view of a large chestnut tree. The attic became the place where Anne would often go to think and be alone.

One of the very first things Anne and her father did was to make rough curtains to hang over the windows. They couldn't risk people outside noticing them. During the day, everyone in the Annex

had to walk barefoot and whisper.
No one could use the toilet or
turn on a tap from
nine o'clock in
the morning to
seven at night.
People working
in the office
building might
hear them. Anne
said everyone was
'as quiet as baby
mice'. Rubbish
was burned in the
stove. This had to
be done after dark because smoke coming out of
the chimney might also attract notice.

It was a cramped space with just the Franks
living there. Then a week later, another family
joined them. They were friends with the

Franks: Mr and Mrs Van Pels and their only child, fifteen-year-old Peter. Peter had brought his cat, Mouschi.

Five months later one more person joined the group: a man named Fritz Pfeffer. Anne thought he was stuffy and boring.

## THE VAN PELS FAMILY

Nevertheless, Anne ended up having to share her room with Mr Pfeffer while Margot moved in with her parents.

Miep was going to be the Franks' main link to the outside world. She was one of four helpers. Besides Miep there was another young woman from the pectin company named Bep, and the two men who now ran Otto's business. Their names were Victor and Johannes. The helpers were putting their own lives at risk, but they would do whatever possible for their friends.

Miep usually came first thing in the morning

FRITZ PFEFFER

BEP VOSKUIJL

**MIEP GIES**

while the offices were still empty. She got the day's shopping list from Anne's mother or from Mrs Van Pels. At lunchtime, she or one of the other helpers would return with the groceries. Miep brought books, newspapers and news of the outside world. Anne was most eager to hear about her friends.

Even though eight people were living so closely together, Anne found the Annex lonely. She and her sister had never been very close. Margot was their mother's pet. She was pretty and intelligent and perfect – and next to her sister Anne felt she always came out second best. But she and Peter van Pels became good friends, and Anne was very happy to have Peter's company. She later developed a crush on him and wrote to Kitty when Peter kissed her for the first time. She wrote, 'I am not alone any more. He loves me, I love him'.

PETER VAN PELS

During the day Anne, Margot and Peter spent a lot of time reading their schoolbooks. Otto Frank helped with their lessons. There was history, literature, foreign languages, geography

and maths. Anne still hated maths. But she
wanted to keep up with her class. So did Margot
and Peter. They all hoped to return to school
very shortly. Later on they taught themselves
shorthand, which is a type of speed writing.

With so many people packed into the Secret
Annex, quarrels broke out. It surprised Anne
that the grown-ups argued so much. Of course,

sometimes the arguments were about Anne. Peter's parents thought she was spoiled. So did Mr Pfeffer. Edith Frank argued with her younger daughter more than ever. But no matter how angry they were at one another, nobody could shout or make a scene. It was too dangerous.

Sometimes at night everyone in the Annex went downstairs to the empty offices. It wasn't the same as going outdoors. But still, Anne could peek out the window and catch sight of people walking on the street.

It was at night, however, that she sometimes felt saddest. She would think about all the things she had lost – her friends, her cat, the feel of sunlight on her skin, the smell of grass and flowers. Anne would pour out her troubles in her diary. She also started writing stories about life in the Annex, stories about her childhood and even fairy tales that she made up.

Days turned into weeks. Weeks turned into

months. Winter came. Anne had been living in the Secret Annex for six months. Now it was dark by four thirty every afternoon. No lights could be turned on inside; they might attract attention. To pass the time, Anne and the others told riddles or talked about books they'd read. They even tried to exercise in the dark.

The boredom was terrible. But being bored was not as bad as the fear of being found. One day there was a knock on the door to the Secret Annex. Was it Nazi soldiers? Was everyone going to be arrested? No! Thankfully it was only one of their helpers. He told them that a carpenter was at work nearby in the offices and not to worry. Another time Peter dropped an enormous twenty-five kilo sack of beans. The sack split open and beans, beans and more beans clattered everywhere. Anne thought that was funny – she was up to her ankles in beans! But making any sort of noise was very risky.

At night the loud sound of aeroplanes could be heard. Anne knew that they were Allied planes, on their way to bomb towns in Germany. The tide of the war had turned against Hitler. Anne's hope was that Germany would surrender – soon. Nevertheless, the noise of the planes frightened her. She would run to her father for comfort. He was the only person in the family who never scolded her. He was always ready to try and calm her.

By spring 1943, food was scarce in the
Netherlands. It became harder and harder for
Miep and the other helpers to bring supplies to
the Annex.

A year had come and gone. Every page in
Anne's diary was filled. But Miep brought more
paper so Anne could continue to write to Kitty.

What Anne would write about had changed. She had become more serious. Her thoughts were often on the war. 'What, oh what, is the use of the war, why can't people live peacefully together . . . ?' she asked Kitty.

Anne herself was changing. She was turning into a young woman. On a wall in her parents' room were little marks that recorded the girls' heights. Anne had grown more than twelve centimetres! Her clothes were much too small for her. Her mind had grown, too. She was no longer a noisy child.

# MIEP AND JAN

MORE THAN ANYTHING, ANNE WANTED MIEP AND HER HUSBAND, JAN, TO SLEEP OVER IN THE ANNEX ONE NIGHT. ON THEIR FIRST ANNIVERSARY, THEY DID.

MANY YEARS LATER, MIEP WROTE A BOOK ABOUT THE FRANKS. IN IT SHE DESCRIBED WHAT THAT NIGHT WAS LIKE. ANNE WANTED THE EVENING TO BE LIKE A GRAND PARTY. SHE HAD SPECIAL MENUS, AND EACH PART OF THE MEAL HAD A FANCY NAME. MIEP SAID THAT SHE AND JAN WERE TREATED AS THOUGH THEY WERE FILM STARS.

THAT NIGHT THEY WERE GIVEN ANNE'S ROOM TO SLEEP IN. THE SECRET ANNEX WAS SO SMALL, MIEP COULD HEAR EVEN THE TINIEST SOUNDS. A SLIPPER DROPPING OR SOMEONE COUGHING IN BED. MIEP CAME TO THE SECRET ANNEX ALMOST EVERY DAY TO SEE HER FRIENDS, AND JAN HAD BEEN THERE MANY TIMES, TOO. BUT LYING THERE IN THE DARK WAS DIFFERENT. MIEP FELT SCARED. ANY LITTLE NOISE STARTLED HER. WAS SOMEONE ABOUT TO BREAK IN? SUDDENLY MIEP BEGAN TO UNDERSTAND WHAT HIDING WAS LIKE. IT WAS FRIGHTENING! AND SHE AND JAN WERE ONLY THERE FOR ONE NIGHT.

Another good thing was that Anne
didn't fight so often with her sister. They
were becoming friends. Anne was also more
understanding towards her mother.

One night, Anne was listening to the radio.
It was a Dutch broadcast from London. The
man said that after the war, diaries and letters

would be published. Anne's dream now was to see her diary turned into a book one day. A book that others would read. She wrote to Kitty, 'You've known for a long time that my greatest wish is to become a journalist someday, and later on a famous writer . . . I want to publish a book entitled *The Secret Annex* after the war; whether I shall succeed or not, I cannot say.'

# Chapter 8
# Caught!

By the time Anne turned fifteen, the families had been in hiding for almost two years – more than 650 days. It was June 1944. The war was drawing to a close. Italy, once an ally of

Germany, had surrendered. The Allied forces were freeing France. On a map pinned to a wall of the Annex, Otto kept track of the Allies' progress. To Anne it was as if friends were approaching. She began looking ahead to freedom.

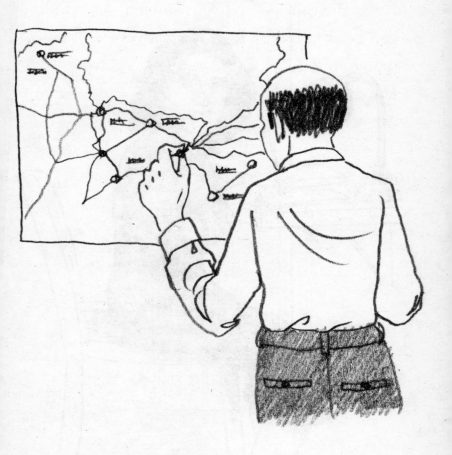

On 15 July 1944, she wrote, 'I think it will all come right, that this cruelty too will end . . . In the meantime I must uphold my ideals, for perhaps the time will come when I shall be able to carry them out!'

# TWO LEADERS

DURING WORLD WAR II, WINSTON CHURCHILL,
THE BRITISH PRIME MINISTER,
AND FRANKLIN D. ROOSEVELT,
PRESIDENT OF THE UNITED
STATES, WERE NOT ONLY UNITED
AGAINST THE GERMANS BUT
BECAME CLOSE PERSONAL
FRIENDS. ROOSEVELT WAS
SERVING HIS THIRD TERM
AS PRESIDENT WHEN THE
UNITED STATES JOINED

**WINSTON CHURCHILL**

THE ALLIED FORCES AT THE END OF 1941. THAT HELPED
TURN THE TIDE OF THE WAR. HE AND CHURCHILL MET
SECRETLY TO COORDINATE THE ATTACKS AGAINST
THEIR COMMON ENEMY. A VICTIM OF POLIO WHO WAS
CONFINED TO A WHEELCHAIR, FRANKLIN ROOSEVELT
IS CONSIDERED ONE OF THE GREATEST AMERICAN
PRESIDENTS EVER. SADLY HE DIED IN APRIL 1945, JUST
MONTHS BEFORE THE WAR ENDED.

**FRANKLIN D. ROOSEVELT**

Then, on the morning of 4 August 1944, Peter heard loud shouting from below. Men's voices. With guns raised, Nazi police stormed the Annex. After so long, after being so careful, they were caught. It was all over.

Someone had betrayed the people in the Secret Annex. But who? To this day, no one knows. Certainly it was not any of their helpers.

After Anne and the others were led away, Miep sneaked into the Annex. She wanted to get there before the Nazis returned to clear everything out. She found Anne's diary on the floor, pages scattered everywhere. Miep gathered them up along with the Frank family photo albums, and locked them in a desk drawer. She hoped that after the war she would be able to return everything to the family.

As for the eight people in the Annex, they all ended up in a concentration camp in Auschwitz, Poland. Otto, Mr Pfeffer, Mr Van Pels and Peter were on the men's side.

Anne, Margot, Edith and Mrs Van Pels went to the women's side.

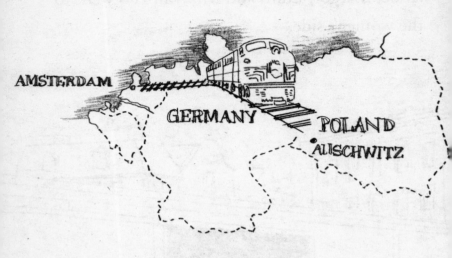

At the camp, most people were put to death straight away – and life for those who weren't could hardly be called life at all. Survivors say it is impossible to describe how awful it was. Margot and Anne were now separated from both their mother and father and moved to a new camp. The girls struggled to survive, but both came down with a sickness called typhus. They died in March 1945.

In April, only one month later, British soldiers arrived and freed everyone left alive in the camp. The war was finally over. But it was too late for Anne Frank.

# Chapter 9
# One Dream Comes True

Of the eight people living in the Annex, only Otto Frank survived the war. He returned to Amsterdam hoping for a family reunion. Instead he learned that his wife and daughters were dead. All that was left were the diary and photographs that Miep had saved.

Otto knew that Anne had kept a diary, but he'd had no idea how much she had written – or how beautiful her words were.

Otto typed up many pages for his mother and friends to read. Everyone urged him to show Anne's diary to publishers. The world needed to hear from this remarkable young girl.

In the summer of 1947, Anne's dream came true: her diary became a book. She was a published author. At first it was called *The Secret Annex*, but later the title was changed to *Anne Frank: Diary of a Young Girl*.

Hitler had murdered six million Jews. That is a fact – a terrible fact – and yet it is almost impossible to understand. Reading about the life of one young girl who died because of Hitler is easier to understand. Anne's diary managed to make a huge, awful event personal. Here was a girl with hopes and dreams. All she had wanted was a chance to live her life.

In the years that followed, Anne's diary became world-famous. It has been translated into more than sixty-five languages. Otto Frank was ninety-one when he died in 1980. He spent those long years keeping alive the memory of Anne and his family.

And he did a very good job. In 1960 the Secret Annex was opened to the public; every year nearly one million visitors visit it. The furniture is gone, but Anne's film star photographs are still on the wall. And visitors see where eight people fought to hold on to their lives in the only way they could – by hiding.

The last words in this book about Anne Frank belong to Anne herself. An optimist to the end, she wrote in one of her final entries, 'In spite of everything I still believe that people are really good at heart'.

# TIMELINE OF ANNE FRANK'S LIFE

1929 —Anne Frank is born on 12 June, in Frankfurt am Main, Germany

1933 —Otto Frank moves to the Netherlands

1934 —Anne and the rest of the family join her father in Amsterdam

1941 —Anne and Margot attend the Jewish School in Amsterdam

1942 —On 12 June Anne receives a diary for her thirteenth birthday; on 6 July the Frank family goes into hiding in the Secret Annex

1944 —In August the residents of the Secret Annex are arrested and sent to concentration camps

1945 —Edith Frank dies on 6 January; Anne and Margot die from typhus in March; Otto Frank returns to Amsterdam on 3 June

1947 —1,500 copies of Anne's diary are published in Amsterdam

1952 —Anne's diary is translated into English

1955 —A play based on *Anne Frank: Diary of a Young Girl* opens on Broadway

1960 —The Secret Annex is opened to the public

# TIMELINE OF THE WORLD

World War I ends — 1918

The Nazi party has its first rally in Munich, Germany — 1923

*The Jazz Singer*, the first non-silent film, opens; — 1927
the New York Stock Market crashes, setting off the
Great Depression

Hitler is appointed Chancellor of Germany; — 1933
Jewish businesses are boycotted; the Gestapo,
or secret police, is formed

The Olympic Games are held in Berlin, Germany; — 1936
Deanna Durbin stars in *Three Smart Girls*

Hitler invades Poland and World War II begins — 1939

The Japanese bomb Pearl Harbor, and the U.S. — 1941
enters World War II

Sophie Scholl of the White Rose is executed — 1943

Hitler kills himself inside a secret bunker; — 1945
Germany surrenders and World War II ends

Princess Elizabeth becomes Elizabeth II, — 1952
Queen of England

Edmund Hillary and Sherpa Tenzing become the first — 1953
people to reach the summit of Mount Everest

John F. Kennedy is elected U.S. president — 1960

# BIBLIOGRAPHY

The books with a * are for younger readers.

Frank, Anne. *Anne Frank: The Diary of a Young Girl.* Doubleday, New York, 1967.

Gies, Miep and Alison Leslie Gold. *Anne Frank Remembered: The Story of Miep Gies, Who Helped to Hide the Frank Family.* Sagebrush Education Resources, Minneapolis, 1988.

Muller, Melissa. *Anne Frank: The Biography.* Henry Holt, New York, 1998.

*Poole, Josephine. *Anne Frank.* Alfred A. Knopf, New York, 2005.

*Pressler, Mirjam. *Anne Frank: A Hidden Life.* Dutton, New York, 2000.

Sawyer, Kem Knapp. *Anne Frank: A Photographic Story of a Life.* DK Publishing, Inc., New York, 2004.

*van der Rol, Ruud and Rian Verhoeven.
*Anne Frank: Beyond the Diary.*
Viking, New York, 1993.

*van Maarsen, Jacqueline. *A Friend
Called Anne.* Viking, New York, 2004.

The website for the Anne Frank
house is www.annefrank.org.

# Your story starts here . . .

Do you **love books** and
**discovering new stories**?
Then **www.puffinbooks.com**
is the place for you . . .

• Thrilling adventures, fantastic fiction
and laugh-out-loud fun

• Brilliant videos featuring your favourite authors
and characters

• Exciting competitions, news, activities,
the Puffin blog and SO MUCH more . . .

**www.puffinbooks.com**